Running Wild

poems by

Patricia McMillen

Finishing Line Press
Georgetown, Kentucky

Running Wild

Copyright © 2024 by Patricia R. McMillen
ISBN 979-8-88838-501-2 First Edition
All rights reserved under International and Pan-American Copyright Conventions. No part of this book may be reproduced in any manner whatsoever without written permission from the publisher, except in the case of brief quotations embodied in critical articles and reviews.

Publisher: Leah Huete de Maines
Editor: Christen Kincaid
Cover Art: iStock "okeyphoto"
Author Photo: Susan Lirakis (@susan.lirakisphoto on IG)
Cover Design: Elizabeth Maines McCleavy

Order online: www.finishinglinepress.com
also available on amazon.com

Author inquiries and mail orders:
Finishing Line Press
PO Box 1626
Georgetown, Kentucky 40324
USA

Contents

Running Wild 1
My Older Sister Teaches Me to Read 2
Smelt Fishing 3
Christmas Eve 1962 5
Pop Sonnet 6
Little Sister 7
Boy Crazy 8
How Not to Drown 9
Gristle 10
Fill-er-Up 11
Illinois 12
Boarding School, 1967 13
To My Period (I) 15
What We Stand For 16
After Finishing College 17
Bazooka Joe Fantasies 18

The Evil Eye 20
The Maid Appears on Queen for a Day 21
Fourth of July, Chicago 23
Who Needs a Heart 24
After Bei Dao 25
January Beach 26
Reveille 27
Wedding 28
That Lonesome Hallway 29
Forgiveness 31
The Truth About Jesus 32
On El Greco's "Assumption of the Virgin" (1627) 33
Windowshopping at the Pink Elephant 34
Barbershop 35
Constant Comment 36
Midwinter Holiday, New Snow 37
To My Period (II) 38

Listening to OCD 40
Baseline Scan 41
Survivor 42
When Blossoms Fall...43
At the Front 44
Love and War 45
To My Period (III)..46
Like Botox for the Brain 47
Outside the AIDS Ward..49
Junior Year/Iraq..50
American Air 51
Hooked 52
Apples to Apples 53
Not three weeks after I marry her widowed father, my new........................55
When We Were a Holy Family 56
Why We Rejected Our Stepmother...57
Time Share At the Dells..59
How I Save My Husband's Life 60
Psalm 2000 61
After Seeing Our Retirement Advisor 62

To My Father, From a Stopped Ski Lift..64
Halloween, San Francisco...65
Tight Wire 66
October 67
The Gods Create Heavy Weather 68
Mayday..69
The Rain Woman...70
Morning on Mars 71
Yang...72
Seven Ways of Listening to a Crow...73
Mrs. Buddha Calls on Mrs. God..74
Square One...75
Sunrise at the Busy Bee Cafe..76

Jesus Heads Home	78
Short Cut	79
Dark Night	80
Notes	81
Acknowledgments	82
Bio	85

Always goin' don't know where
Always showin', I don't care
Don't love nobody, it's not worth while
All alone, runnin' wild. Runnin' wild!

—Joe Grey and Leo Wood, "Running Wild" (1922 Song)

For Jack, always

Running Wild

A young girl, I gallop the green lawn,
she-centaur, child of cloud: my proud
mane streaming, reins in one fist, riding crop
landing hard. I give myself new names: Shy Anne
and Percival, Rufus, Sir Mac. I know

real horses, I've flicked away real flies
at my grandmother's farm; have worn
my sister's riding helmet, black knee boots,
her canary jodhpur pants. I have held
the dented can of saddle soap, used bits
of kitchen sponge to make lather. I've smelled

real smells: manure mixed with hay, rain-wet
leather, men's sweat. Yet I prefer
these afternoons of being a wagon team
all by myself, harness jingling as I turn
a wide arc—of being, when I will, a whole herd.

My Older Sister Teaches Me to Read

Margot says the first thing I must learn
is what I'm eating, from the yellow box.
The name starts with a *C* plus *H*, which makes
a sound like *choo-choo.* Then an *E,* plus *E*
makes "long E"—*eek!,* or *Whee!* or *teevee,* where
I've seen the "Kid" who shills this stuff—then *R,*
for *robin, Rumpelstiltskin, Rice-a-Roni,*

which makes what? *CHEER-,* like cheer up, cheer-
ful cheerleader—that dream I'll never be, though she
can turn a row of perfect cartwheels on the street
in front of our suburban stucco house—
though from this breakfast table, it seems sure
one day she'll float up Cherry Street on
a Chevelle convertible—green, with white
rag top, our high school's colors—instead
of shipping off to girls' school, leaving me

alone to rummage through her dresser drawers
rattling with half-empty nail polish bottles,
to puzzle through her castoff Shakespeare plays
unguided. But pre-rupture, I'm her rapt
captive, entranced at how this dotted *I*'s
pronounced—like double *E*—and reach the *O,*
for *Oh, oat doughnuts floating in a bowl*;
then *S:* for *sister, sneeze,* and for *straight* from
the cardboard box, the way we like them best.

Smelt Fishing

—for Dad

By flashlight, by Coleman lantern we fish—
God, my father and me—out past my bedtime
with some of his friends
at the end of the concrete pier.

Before us the hard rutted
road of moonlight, behind us
the power plant's square yellow windows,
night-shift boys blowing smoke rings
and watching us, and

I am the only girl.

And the men throw furled nets
into black water, roll them back
heavy with silver.
It is my job to empty the nets,

crouched beside Dad's huge
unbuckled boot, untangling
each tiny gill from the cording,
trying not to hurt the fish. I wear

my sister's old pea-green velour
ski jacket, the one Mom refuses to wash,
saying the scales
would wreck her machine,
so it gleams with history—

and when Dad says "Hurry up"
I do, tearing
the fish from the net, flinging them
two by two into the galvanized
metal pail until at last,
my fingers numb, he

unties the weights, rolls
the nets, packs everything
into the station wagon. Then we head
uphill, towards home,

and I doze, dreaming
of their little black eyes

Christmas Eve 1962

My father, kneeling, spreads a strand of lights
across the living room wall-to-wall, unscrews
each bulb in turn and shakes it, frowns, until
at last he finds the burned-out one and twists

a new bulb in, and the whole string—red, green,
orange, blue, yellow—blinks on. Mom puts down
her sewing, cheers and claps, as Mimi smiles
from Daddy's chair. I play "Joy to the World",

downward through the white keys, on the piano.
All fall I've pasted savings stamps in books
to trade for teddy bears for my boy cousins.
I haven't peeked at tags on gifts hidden

on the sunporch—I even feign belief in Santa Claus
for my four-year-old sister's sake—but one day soon,
when it's my turn, I'll ask: why didn't Mimi clap
for me? where are my Jewish friends tonight?

And JFK will die, Negroes will mass in our suburb,
demand the righting of unfathomable wrongs.
The frail membrane of my childhood will tear,
a jagged hole not even Mom can mend.

Pop Sonnet

That year when Daddy gives me a new black
transistor radio just like his but
with my name, not his, scotch-taped to the back,
and breastless in my blue bathing suit
I walk to the beach with a rolled-up towel
and my two best friends, both brunettes who turn
soy sauce brown to my raw-red-and-freckled
though we share one bottle of Coppertone—
on WLS, it's Biondi
spinning "Baby Love," "Wendy, What Went Wrong?"—
every three minutes, a new tragedy.
Sharing a Coke three ways, bopping along,
harmonies wafting skyward on our dreams,
who's to tell us we aren't the next Supremes?

Little Sister

When I think how close I came
to losing you in the Monadnock Building
after my first eye doctor appointment,
Mom and I both stunned to hear him say
I needed glasses—would I never
dance Swan Lake?—both crying, waiting
for the elevator which though classy

had no operator, was uncomprehending
as a toaster or neuro-ophthalmologist,
and when it came, how you hopped right on
while we stood, watched those ornate
glass-and-brass doors bang shut, eight-year-old
you on one side with your pixie haircut,
Mom and thirteen-year-old me on the other:

O then did I become a woman, then know
what loss would be, and when, that same lifetime,
Mom and I still paralyzed on the seventh floor,
the same doors clanged open again, revealing you
untouched, unharmed, valiant in the elevator cab,

O then did we three keen in tragic unison
all the way out to Jackson Boulevard.

Boy Crazy

If it wasn't this one, copping
a feel beside the rusty
wheelbarrow in my father's garage,
then that one, maybe, leaning in
for the kiss but first bending to pull
up socks that had slipped down
inside his shoes while I sat there
feeling foolish in too much lip gloss
on a stone bench behind the bowling alley
the weekend after Kennedy was shot.

How Not to Drown

—after Hal Sirowitz

Don't go swimming right after lunch,
Mother said. Wait at least twenty
minutes, or better yet, an hour. Otherwise
you'll get cramps, you'll fold up like
an ironing board & when you breathe
your lungs will fill with water & you'll
drown unless somebody gets you an
ambulance like that time you were three,
you didn't know how to swim & you ran
straight into Lake Michigan to meet your
father who was walking in after swimming
back and forth across the horizon so far
out we could hardly see him. Lucky for you
he was paying attention, he got to you just
in time because that kid up on the life-guard
chair didn't even notice. That's how boys are:
too busy flirting with some girl in a skimpy
two-piece. As for me, of course I was watching,
but you know I don't like to get my hair wet.

Gristle

A man remembers looking
at a girl's hair under a microscope,
still remembers how the colors
split into a rainbow. After eighth grade
ended, and high school, and college,
he went to law school because science
was too heartbreaking.

Another remembers kissing a girl
behind the black-and-white TV set
in her mother's formica kitchen. He's
a fertility doctor now, obsessed
with the dancing forms of infinitely
small humans.

And another remembers traveling
to the city with a girl and her mother
for the children's symphony, how
on the way back home, he and the girl
held up home-made signs in the back
window: "Honk if you love chocolate!"
Later he fell for an exotic dancer,
and later still, filed for bankruptcy.

A fourth man, now a ski instructor, remembers
how his father read him stories at night,
inserting a real girl's name for the frog,
pig, bear. "Jump over the moon, said
Susie O'Brien," is what he remembers,
his father's voice still strong then, he himself
wearing those brown Roy Rogers pajamas.

Fill-'er-Up

It wasn't like it is now. In those days,
when marriages split, you knew one or both
of them was helpless drunk or queer. Their shades

stayed drawn all day, their kids drank beer, smoked pot,
got hooked on comic books. Even Tootsie,
their old black Lab, slumped past full garbage cans,

ashamed. It meant the whole community
had failed. No telling what might happen next:
geese could fly north, air raid sirens get stuck

mid-blast. At Gary's Gas, men laid their cards
down, fell silent, when *she* pulled to the pump,
cut the engine. Gary (whose own affair

lay twenty years ahead, how could he know?)
would wish he'd someplace else to go, but sigh,
wipe those huge hands across smudged coveralls,

step to the driver's side as—slowly, too—
she cranked the window down. Like it or not,
back then—back then, full service was a job.

Illinois

Another ten, fifteen, two hundred miles
down the highway there'll be something to see—
The Dixie Buffet Café, Mother Jones' grave—
but here, where two roads cross, there's not so much

as a red-winged blackbird. Nothing doing
even on the car radio: sermons gave way
an hour back to static and road noise.
Cars float on a square-cornered, wakeless lake

of soybean acreage—parallel crop rows,
train tracks, fencing, with here and there a slash
of transmission lines looping *woo-woo-woo*
between donkey-eared delta pylons—float

past State prison, somebody's Grandma's house.
Fifty miles past that is the horizon.
Out here everything's orderly, like it
should be everywhere. Orange-jumpsuited men

pack trash in big black plastic bags, leave them
spaced on the roadside *bing-bing-bing*. Scanning
distances measured by telephone poles,
a person might say "stasis," might say "death"—

or might say "home." Because there's something here
no one can take away: faithful wood posts
standing upright as uncles after church,
straight as country aunts, arms outstretched in prayer.

Boarding School, 1967

Thanksgiving weekend: my folks say it's too
expensive to fly me home, pawn me off
on a cousin in Dedham. She's only nine
years older, but married, tries to boss me.
Saturday I go downtown, smoke menthols,

lean against Filene's, my forest green
polyester blend maxicoat wrapped over
a lavender miniskirt, fishnet-stockinged legs.
I'm thinking "It's fucking cold in Boston,"
and how that's got a sound I like: "it's *fucking*

cold." If I had paper, I could write it down,
send it to my best friend, back in Illinois,
who right now is smoking pot in someone's
parents' basement or riding around
in someone's red Mustang, eight-track of Sgt.

Pepper's in the tape deck, *She's leaving home,
bye bye*—but I don't even have a fucking pen.
God, how I hate Boston, hate boarding school,
hate every East Coast stranger rushing past
as daylight fades: long-haired greasers in black

leather jackets, women with huge day-glo
peace-symbol earrings. I finish my last
Newport, stub it out, and then I'm in
the store, stuffing a pair of pantyhose,
patent leather heels, bag of Charleston Chews

into my plastic daisy print tote bag,
and back on the sidewalk before I'm busted—
which gets me out of school, but only for
three fucking days. No one can understand
why I would shoplift: don't I want to go

to college? On Monday, Mom arrives.
We meet with the headmistress, then call Dad.
Tuesday Mom takes me to Gone With the Wind,
the 70mm re-release, then out for ice cream.
It's something, I guess—not that I fucking care.

To My Period (I)

I remember clearly the first time we met,
on an airplane in 1967. I was fifteen,
on a trip with my mother. After we landed, I hid
in the guest room of her friend's house
while Mom asked our hostess—who had a son my age—
if she had an extra sanitary napkin and belt.

After that you went away for a few months
but you came back,
and that was the end of childhood.
You made yourself at home between my legs,
bringing your strange smells and cravings,
making me morose and poetic
sometimes even before lunch.
You brought other baggage, too:

the swollen breasts, the not sleeping
on my stomach, the not sleeping at all; there was
the part about disappointment, the part about not
being a mother again this time. You and your
intractability, your mysteriousness stranger
than Holy Communion! At times I understood
why women became pagan
and danced around bonfires.

It was you, not the Serpent,
who made us into witches
and men into inquisitors.

What We Stand For

She said *I don't believe our ancestors
crossed the Atlantic, ate hard tack, wore
scratchy underwear just so you could
lie on the couch and talk on the phone
all day.* She said *We're part English.
We don't wear stripes with plaids, don't
swing our hips, we hide our teeth
when we smile. We have pale skin,
blue eyes, a tendency to develop moles
after the age of thirty. It's nothing
to be ashamed of.* She said *We're part
English, part Scottish, part French—
direct descendants of Louis the Some-
teenth. (I don't care for genealogy,*
she said. *All those begats.)* She said
*Your great-great-grandfather invented
the piano bench.* Said *It's okay to have
Jewish friends, I have one myself, but
don't bring them home, you know how
it upsets your father.* Said *Of course
we gave you piano lessons, but we didn't
want you to become a musician.* Said
Not right now, Said *Take your feet off
the coffee table,* Said *Sit up straight,* Said
Whatever else you do, finish college first.

After Finishing College

Mother writes checks for the psychiatrist,
then over meatloaf asks me what I said
about her. Doctor H has the long head,
sad eyes of a basset. His son's a pest

I knew in grammar school. I don't feel like
talking but I tell him how I threw
a cup of coffee at her wall. It flew
crooked, hit the ceiling. "You won't make

my ball team," he jokes, trying to play
but I grimace, refuse. The truth is I've read
Phyllis Chesler, I'm convinced that if I said
what I thought, they'd lock me away.

As for Freud's *dictum*–"to love and to work"—
what's to love about the date who grinds
his hard-on into my spine, who finds
my grief amusing? Freaked out, spiral-bound,

I scrawl notes for poems, claw my way up
until I'm ready for a retail gig.
 "I'm fine," I say, cram notebooks into big
white bags, leave them for the garbage truck.

Bazooka Joe Fantasies

Comic #34 of 50:
in this one, Zena dreams she's on a date
with Johnny Depp, but not the Depp we know:

this one's crosseyed, his skin hot cartoon pink,
his hair a mess. *Zena, I want to say,
dreams are always like this: always both more*

and less than we desire. Teenaged girls dream
mothers deaf to dream-sobs; for ex-wives, it's
ex-husbands winning bullfights, bloody ears

between clenched teeth. *Zena, I want to say,
listen, there are no perfect loves—only
perfect strangers, and even they have flaws.*

She can't hear me, but she'll come out OK:
when Depp asks "Will I see you pretty soon?"
she nails him: "Don't you think I'm pretty now?"

The Evil Eye

—for M.C.

This my grandmother taught me, this
the priest does not deny: at daybreak,
take a single egg from the brown hen.

Do not look into the eyes of the bird
(this brings bad luck). Pass the egg
three times before the afflicted

one, each time repeating the words
of the Apostles' Creed: holy spirit,
holy church, holy resurrection

of the flesh. Do not look into
the eyes of the afflicted one (this
causes transfer of the evil eye

to you). Now break the egg
into a glass of water. The evil eye,
see how it floats to the top?

Leave the glass on a table for three
days, then empty it onto the ground
outside a kitchen door. When your first

daughter comes of age, teach this
to her. Teach her, also, to pray daily
to the Virgin, who will sustain her.

The Maid Appears on Queen for a Day

Just before show time, Your Host Jack Bailey
asks Makeup "Who's on today?" "Usual
hard luck in housecoats, plus a strange one—frail,
foreign. Doesn't look pregnant." Furrowed frown,
glides the eyebrow pencil. "But you're a pro.
She'll be in tears before commercials roll"—

slides Jack's rug into place. It's true: Jack's got
the knack to make a whole nightclub cry. Ask
a girl what her husband does—what he *did*,
before he lost his job. Pump the pity,
but don't break Rule One: Sponsors Don't Like
Surprises.—Down the hall, a network page

presses one ear to a dressing room door,
hears a mumbled name "Michael." Softly knocks.
"They're ready for you, honey." Trouser-clad,
the girl emerges, takes her seat onstage.
She says her name is Joan, and she's fifteen.
Kids, husband? Shakes for "no." Her gaze upturned,

Joan speaks not to the audience, nor host,
but to the lights. Jack keeps it low-key, smooth,
but by break, the girl's unbroken. "Sweetheart,"
he says, as Makeup powders his cheekbones.
"I'll give you one last chance. Next take,
share your pain with the folks at home, or you're

gone without so much as a toaster." Lights
up, we're back, and the girl, unblinking, speaks:
"Give me horses, an army's worth of men."
Finger across his throat, Jack makes the "kill" sign.
Three singers warble jingles offstage left
while Makeup readies the next guest.

That night, the page will tell his mother how
he helped the poor girl out: sashayed her through
an alley exit, over to Sunset,
slipped her two bucks, saw her into a cab.
How, as the strange girl settled into place,
light from a thousand suns shone in her face.

Fourth of July, Chicago

My mother told me "Lie down with dogs,
stand up with fleas." That's why at first I'm glad
to find his place is overrun with cats:

Persian, calico, tortoise, Manx, draped
like antimacassars across the arms
of rescued Victorian sofas, dozing

on windowsills, play-batting dustballs.
Salsa music rises from Clark Street, a pulse
as sullen as heat, drifts through the open window

on a breeze smelling of tortillas and yesterday's
diesel exhaust. He's beating me, slowly,
at strip chess. I lose a bishop, take

off one sock, lick salt from my upper lip.
Sweat rolls from my scalp, lodges in a brow.
He's sweet, I think, sweet—but I'm so hip,

I've got no time for love, only enough
to tangle on a frayed bedspread covered
with cat hair, while far off, a lost dog howls.

Who Needs a Heart

In the front room a dead ficus,
each dry branch perfectly intact,

trembles to the bass line: *what's love
got to do, got to do with it?*

Two rooms back, we argue—*what's love?*—
then sleep. He's got every reason

not to trust me. *A second hand
emotion.* I won't loose my grip

from the rail, won't skate to mid-rink,
know all I care to know about

falling. Outside, more snow. A crowd
gathers, smokes cigarettes, before

going inside to talk the talk.
We argue—*what's love?* Then we sleep.

After Bei Dao*

A man offers me an umbrella at a bus stop
and I accept. Later I tell this story at work
and all the secretaries laugh, because
it isn't raining.

(In Hawaii, sea climbs a cliff.)

Women waiting in line outside public bathrooms
or eating chocolate-dipped strawberries from sticks.
Women stepping over puddles of spilled beer.

(In Chicago, a midnight swim.)

When lightning strikes a bird's nest
every young mother hears sirens.
There are feathers on the ground,
blood, bones in the air.
The sky is very dark.

(In Jerusalem, a bullet-scarred doorway.
In Paris, soft air across a girl's shoulders.)

When will he stop promising roses?
Are there no other beautiful flowers?
When will he tell me the truth?

*(A fake translation from the Chinese)

January Beach

Under pink skies a clutch of white balloons,
breakwater-buttressed, rests like refugees
from someone's Sweet Sixteen. Above, paired geese
float motionless as tarnished silver spoons.
I pick a path through pop-tops, bent tire rim,
spent shotgun shell, fragment of cobalt glass,
avoiding shadows where teen lovers kiss.
They won't escape love's undertow this time.

Last night I heard the story of a bride
who posed for pictures on a coastal cliff.
Hair flowing, hoop skirt belled with breeze, she smiled
and smiled as, from behind, an ocean swelled,
swallowed her whole.—Warnings fade at twilight:
NO GUARD ON DUTY/SWIM AT YOUR OWN RISK.

Reveille

God at my window every morning

tapping a bare black branch, break-
dancing through my dream of endless

winter, then one day showing up
wearing lace: a wedding dress.

Yesterday a cobalt sky, today
dead white—is this

another of Your practical jokes?—

while hidden from view, diligent sparrows
practice songs in their sleep.

Wedding

>—*after Czeslaw Milosz, "Encounter"*

We stood in a chapel as daylight faded.
A minister spoke gently,

and suddenly my knees trembled.
No one felt this except me.

It seems long ago. Today we are here,
alone in our house, far from the little chapel.

O my love, where will we go next?
The shutting of a book; a glance; a cough.
I ask, not knowing the answer.

That Lonesome Hallway

I.

What's left of his breakfast
sloshes in a kidney-
shaped pan, vomit stained red
by the cranberry juice

he drank with his oatmeal.
Over the shaver's buzz
I hear him tell the nurse
he smokes half a pack a

day, though just last night he
swore to me, again, he'd
quit. As sick as he is,
I want to kill him.

II.

In the park, a mounted
policeman stops to talk.
I rub the horse's neck,
inhaling the scent like

incense. I want to tell
someone how, this morning,
my husband's face turned gray
as a sidewalk. Instead

I watch while Rex (the horse)
sticks his whole head, bridle
and all, into the trough,
exhaling bubbles.

III.

Every morning, a black-
robed priest offers him
what I cannot: forgiveness,
a dry wafer. As he

recovers, we walk the wards,
each day coming a little
closer to the plaster saint
that guards each hallway.

Next week we'll head
for Jesus, Who waits,
ribcage torn open,
red heart in one hand.

Forgiveness

is a hard woman insisting I spend
New Year's Day writing an apology to her boyfriend

for things I don't recall saying the night before, and if I did—
hell, he was drunk too. Holding up my karma as if she had

a direct line, knew even half
the things I've done wrong: breezing past

Salvation Army Santas, my pockets full of quarters; that day
I told the boss I was sick but just wanted to stay

home and watch TV; the sheepdog pup
I kicked. Forgiveness—ah,

forgiveness: how I wish her love were sap
that never stopped flowing, that I could tap

her like a maple tree in winter, set
my empty bucket at an angle, let

not a single drop of her sweetness run
off, flow away, across the frozen ground.

The Truth About Jesus

Her sudden death at home redeemed our shame-
filled nudges, whispers rustling as she'd rise,
mid-sermon, apoplectic, to proclaim
"Jesus had a twin brother!"—her wild eyes
rolled heavenward. Now one man mourns a wife,
but we raise hopes for Resurrection Day,
our love writ large into the Book of Life.
And now the church is quiet when we pray,
save for her father, who each week still wears
the same worn suit, sits in the same wood pew
under the window in which Christ suffers
the little children, mutters softly through
communion, and on leaving, reaches up
to touch the crack in Jesus' stained-glass foot.

On El Greco's "Assumption of the Virgin" (1627)

Men gathered at the open tomb ignore
that woman hanging just above their heads,
continue to debate politics, trade

gossip earth-bound as dirt. Not that she needs
their countenancing, their approval: no,
her life was not to serve them, though she served

their purposes. Now, ever-rising in her painted
red velvet nightgown and bare feet, it's
goodbye to Midwestern schoolchildren

who kneel beside a wood gallery bench,
pencils sharpened, answering fifteen
multiple choice questions; goodbye, guard,

leaning in a doorway, watching me write,
as once it was goodbye to dazzled Toledo
worshipers. Toes wrapped around a yellow moon,

Mary ascends to Heaven, where, as Queen,
she'll breathe secrets into God's good ear, bring home
more than a guess at next year's fashion trends.

Windowshopping at The Pink Elephant

Stopped cuckoo clocks and cracked Depression glass,
worn one-eyed teddy bears that every day
get bought and sold, appear and disappear—
I'm walking past, not stopping, when my ear

picks out a strangled beat, lonely descant
of one seal barking on a rocky coast.
Through the window my eyes search for the sound,
past rows of beat-up secretaries to

a back brick wall, where the tired fiftyish
shopkeeper stands, black mascara blurred, face
flushed the neon pink of the elephant
buzzing over her head. In one hand

she clutches the gauze curtain which most days
hides the shop's interior from the street.
A man slumps, forlorn, under her elbow.
She gestures—I can't glean her words—and then

it dawns on me, how her mouth, opening
and closing, matches the staccato bark
of the imagined seal. I stand watching,
sure what I'm feeling now is what our young

newly-wed neighbors did when you and I
lived in your townhouse, those long nights we drank
too hard, *goddamns* landing like slaps. I duck
before I'm noticed, rush to catch my train.

Hours later, headed home, I pass the shop
again. The street's silent. One sleepless bear
waves sadly through the window. At his back,
the white veil dangles on its crooked wire.

Barbershop

Fritz finishing his four o'clock: a whiff
of talc. Three empty chairs, toilet in back,
Miguel pushing a broom. Already it's
gone dark outside. Fritz and his five o'clock
talk about Johnny, shot dead at Smith's Gas,
two blocks away. Johnny's father was there
but now he's scared to talk to the police
after those punks threatened to torch his car.
Fritz says "Shows they knew him. Must be locals"—
like us. Like Johnny. Flourishes the cloak:
"You're next." Outside, gently, a clean snow falls.
"You hear about that lady from Burr Oak?
Car-jacked, left for dead off US 80."
It figures. Christmas makes us all crazy.

Constant Comment

Thirty years later, I know now that he
was never angry, never blamed me—as
I even, sometimes, blamed myself. But he
never judged. Yet, each morning, when he'd lift
his morning-heavy head from the pillow,
place one foot, then the other, on the bare
wood floor, saying nothing—nothing at all—
pull blue jeans over knees, buckle his belt,
creak down the stairs to start our tea—I'd hear
it all, each word he didn't say, until
the kettle sighing, he'd open the lid
of the wooden tea box, find it empty.
Then I'd feel—he'd nowhere else to put it—
the full weight of his mute disappointment.

Midwinter Holiday, New Snow

At the quaint Frisco inn with mountain views
I bleed all morning in a queen size bed
until he tells me to get up. He wants
to ski. We go downstairs, where our hostess

offers bowls, granola, milk, then settles
with her two-year-old in the living room,
folding laundry in front of the TV.
We drive to town, not talking much, and park

outside the ski rental place, where halfway
through filling out a form (age: thirty-nine,
experience: average), checking the box
to release liability, the cramps

get worse. I excuse myself, weave between
racks of neon pink ski pants and parkas
to a ladies' room behind a cheap oak
laminate partition. Last Tuesday, when

the ultrasound showed no fetal heartbeat,
the blunt nurse handed me a plastic vial,
two latex gloves, the number of a lab
in Pueblo. I pull the gloves on now, squat

over the bowl. This isn't what I had
in mind: where's his nervous grin, his teary
gratitude as our firstborn crowns? Instead,
one last swirl of rhododendron red

in water, and I've caught it: an inch-long
effigy, crude-carved of yellow gristle,
an armless, eyeless, lifeless artifact
my womb has spit out. Vial capped, I zip

my pocket closed, and when the pains subside,
find him waiting, with his skis. "I've got it,"
I say, though we both know we're not driving
to Pueblo. Not when we've got new snow.

To My Period (II)

The first time you showed up, I thought you were kind of cool
in your leather jacket and sideburns,
though you gave me a headache and made me thirsty.

Maybe you thought I was proud to have you,
and maybe I was at first,
but it didn't take long before you became a nuisance,
inviting yourself to movie dates and swimming parties,
barging in on doctor's appointments,
even pushing your way back mid-pregnancy
with a face that scared away babies, and who could blame them?
(My lovers never liked you, either,
for their own reasons.)

Once you surprised me at work,
though it wasn't my birthday. You interrupted a meeting
and wrecked my skirt. After that
I searched everywhere for another skirt
to match that jacket, but the ones I found
were never quite right.

Listening to OCD

Since Prozac I can't
keep the spice jars in
alphabetical

order. There's a stack
of receipts for car
repairs on one end

table, unopened
mail on the other.
I forget people's

zip codes, even the
names of their cats. Nights
I dream of pushing

a grocery cart
with one bent wheel, of
ironing men's shirts

over and over
under a full moon,
while some days, I read

magazines without
clipping recipes,
I let milk go sour.

Baseline Scan

After a morning at Nuclear Medicine where the X-ray guy
and I discuss his recent pituitary gland surgery
(they went in under his upper lip, which is still sore)
and whether there will be war
in Iraq, I'm hungry and it's raining and a lot
of people have black umbrellas out
but I don't have one, while others line up for
caramel corn which honestly has never

appealed to me so I go looking for a book by Langston
Hughes, anything really, walking maybe fifteen
blocks south to the public library to see what he
thought (though his war was different), checking carefully
at each corner even when the walking man
signal comes on because, God knows, accelerators can
stick and that's not even to mention
that more and more people every day

careen around city streets in barely disguised versions
of military vehicles permitting little or no peripheral vision
and although I get wet, really kind of soaked
except for my feet which somehow manage to stay dry
I keep thinking about how the X-ray guy
said I was his second client in one day to call the President
a "loose cannon"—which is why he likes his job, *it's
the people*—and, as I zipped

my jeans, how he handed me at no extra charge
prints of one screen showing my left hip
and a second one showing four of my vertebrae, each accompanied
by plus or minus variances and computer-plotted
graphs and said it looked like everything was OK
though he wasn't a doctor, and how
I folded the prints into my backpack and thanked him and moved on,
feeling strangely proud of the density of my bones.

Survivor

What I meant by "lonely" was nothing
I could name exactly—a tinfoil crackle
always in my ear, a taste somewhere
between dust and battery acid—something

my sisters didn't understand. What I meant
by "dead" wasn't literally "dead," either,
more a way of not feeling at home even in
the place I still called "home," even in

my body. Maybe it was a process, driving
from one place to the next, rescued mutt
in the back seat, gallon Ziploc of dog biscuits
in my lap. Maybe the looking for a sign,
a white H on a blue background not because
I needed medical attention but because that's

where the pay phones were. Maybe the stopping
to call back to the last county, find out if he
was still behind me and if so how far. Maybe
the effort to stay calm by singing with the radio
or maybe it was somehow knowing I'd never again
sit at our kitchen table looking out at the cherry tree

in bloom, knowing that while there wouldn't
be the same kind of fear—words hissed in
anger, dishes thrown against cabinet doors—
neither would there be the same kind of spring.

So it was that I held that taste under my tongue
for years until the night I crept from our bed,
slant light from the hall closet
barely enough to see to tie my shoes.

When Blossoms Fall

In this season when white flowers fall
like paper rosebuds from the hands of trees
to decorate the hoods of cars that loll
on city curbsides—once again, love, we
will separate, and this time it may be
forever. There has been nothing but rain
this month, rain and more rain. The storms shake free
these blossoms like so many blessings strewn
by giant creatures reaching, so like us,
crooked arms to the sky. Muscogee named
them winged heads—"*catalpa*"—but I see skulls
bursting, like yours, like mine, into white flame.
Ah! how is love, that thing so old, so new,
so easy to start, painful to undo?

At the Front

So this is war. That explosion you heard
    was no landmine—only a thought balloon
that hovered, cloudlike, until I pricked it,
    spitting punctuation, partial sentences
like shrapnel into the flesh of sister,
    father, husband. No, don't say "She means well."
As purple crocuses burst into bloom, he takes
    a furnished room downtown, leaves me
the house. I resettle his things—bowling trophies,
    golf clubs, shotgun—in refugee camps
under the basement stairs. Neighbors offer
    solace but it's like they're talking
to an image on their TV screens. "Too late
    to refuel now," I say. "We're going down."

Love and War

> *"and so my love, once unashamed and senseless, has fallen far away, like an arrow shot from a bow." – Kuruntokai 231, ascribed to Pālai pātiya Perunkatunko, Tamil poet ca. 4 c. BCE*

In a faraway suburb, reading
poetry of a faraway time,

I imagine him, planning his new
kitchen while downtown, his lawyer
files the case *Him vs. Me*

and I wait for someone new, someone
I hope will be entirely unlike him
though it's too soon to tell.

I think, too, of his mother,
who persisted in her love
against all common sense
—yet who can say?

The sadness of the archer, letting go
the pulsing string; the hard fall of the doe.

To My Period (III)

After my first divorce, you stalked me
like an ex-husband. You showed up at night clubs,
inspecting your fingernails at the edge of the dance floor
while I flirted with a new love interest,
shouldering him aside at the worst
possible moment. "Sorry," you'd say,
"I saw her first."

These days you show up later and later
as if finally starting to take the hint
that you were unwelcome from the start.
Go then! begone!
and take that half-empty
bottle of hydrogen peroxide
with you when you leave. Little by little,
my sweating and forgetfulness
will pass. After that I won't miss you,
nor shopping in the "feminine hygiene" aisle.

Like Botox for the Brain

—for Dr. K.

"Relax," says the psychiatrist. "What's the use
of worrying about people as they drink
themselves slowly to death? It's none
of your business. And who even cares it's
Christmas?"—a season that (he knows)
makes me some combination of sad and
ticked off with its noise and commotion,
O Holy Nights and Little Drummer Boys

racing around in my head after nothing
more than a simple trip to Walgreens
for dental floss. But this year it's like
all the fight's sucked out of me
and I can't argue with him. I, who once
could argue with anyone about anything—
now when I meet an acquaintance
on the train platform, and he launches

his usual tirade of grievances (concealed
carry, fluoride, his sinuses), I beam,
I pat his arm, I say "Good to see you!"
and walk away. Like a sponge diver
in a big copper helmet, I'm on the ocean
floor, my emotions forming like air bubbles,
expanding so slowly I can identify them
and watch them float to the surface.

I tell myself this is a new kind of happiness
but maybe it's a substitute for happiness
as napping is a substitute for sleeping at night
and sleeping at night is a substitute for dreaming
and this psychiatrist is a substitute for a friend
who listens without being paid. But
"It's only money," says the psychiatrist,
"and besides not every friend gives you drugs

so you can dive deep, hunker down where
it's quiet and let your insane bloated worries—
the ones you've lived with so long
they are like family members, distant
half-cousins who moved in after
their marriages failed—hover in silence."
Through a rasp of air hose, faint echo
of Silver Bells, I can almost hear them pop.

Outside the AIDS Ward

—in memoriam Phillip M. (1950-1990)

Death slouches in the waiting room,
skimming *People* magazine,
      toying with a lock of hair,
clicking long black fingernails
      on the armrests of the plastic chair.

An electronic waterfall
      drips on fake geraniums.
Death bites at a cuticle,
bops to Creedence, spits skin tags
      onto yellow-waxed linoleum.

Immortal in their grainy smiles,
benefactors on the wall
      train on Death their sightless eyes.
Even she can't stare them down—
      a puny victory for puny Man.

At last the bearded medic nods,
      the dusty nurse with icy hands
disconnects the morphine drip.
      A high hat masks the patient's sigh.
Death stretches her stiff limbs and slowly stands.

Junior Year/Iraq

Here: walking from class to the library,
from the dorm to class, fear like sunlight
filtered through clouds, swelling,
diminishing. There: dust, wind,

a reporter wearing night-vision glasses
talking about what he could or could
not disclose as to his location. There:
bombs popping in a green-tinted sky; close-up

of a guy who might have been my next-door
neighbor sending greetings home to "Nicole,"
to "Mom." Here: interviews of "Nicole,"
of "Mom," not crying or crying only a little.

Here: sitting in the student lounge
watching a plasma screen, drinking a Diet
Coke, trying to be grateful for my freedom,
not knowing really how to feel.

American Air

Headed for sunset, girls in camouflage
play hearts across the aisle, their steel-toed boots
identical to those of the young men
seated beside them watching Bruce Willis

and Mos Def on laptops. How new they look,
the boys almost more fragile than the girls,
all grateful as a steward passes out
pretzels and 7-Ups—and all so clean,

as though grooming won wars. At SFO
we amble past displays marked "Natural
History": bleached swordfish, shark-tooth knives,
fugu floating in formaldehyde.

I feign interest while trying not to think
how much I pay these kids to kill for me,
these sons and daughters who will come home
mangled, crumpled, their scrubbed faces gone.

Hooked

The car is small, its windows stuck open, swallowing wind, swallowing rain. Lightning cracks. The steering wheel bucks her grip like a graphite fishing pole with two hundred pounds of bigeye on the wire, two hundred pounds of sheer fight.

She's blonde now; if this is fun, she's having more of it. She blinks, and the rain turns to hail, to sleet, to snow. Eyes open: no visibility. The road signs covered with ice, unreadable.

She's thinking about their last argument. "You have to understand the difference between disorder and chaos," he'd said. Impossible, she thought, to argue with a philosopher, but she'd try anyway: "I know all about chaos; the insane number of vectors." Well, didn't she?

She lets go of the steering wheel. The tires spin, the car caroms from one shoulder to the other. The radio went silent twenty miles ago, but when she hits a bump, it springs on again: Tommy James, soloing, *My baby does the hanky pank—*. One last plucked guitar string before the radio dies again, Shondells silenced at their microphones.

What state is this anyway? All this snow—maybe it's Canada. Frozen fish fly through the air—squid, smelt, rigid as old priests. His voice echoes in her brain: "After she died, all I had to do at night was sleep." Where's her gaff, her dehooker? She presses the accelerator to the floor, yanks the wheel left, then right.

The snow turns to rain; the rain slows, then stops. Bycatch clearing, she spots a sign: **MEMPHIS, 10 MILES.**

It's the wrong exit. She takes it anyway.

Apples to Apples

*Your love was an apple
yet even after death
she consumes you.*

How heavy are the hats and sweaters of the departed
in the closets of the living. How heavy,
heavy as tombstones
in the closets of the bereaved.
How heavy is the heart of my beloved
who is filled with grief.

*Grief is the red red apple of love. Grief
hangs from the low branch
heavy with scent. Grief wears the face,
sings the song of the kitchen clock:*
tick tock, tick tock, *give in, give in.*

He is wrapped in grief
as in a sweater. On warm
days, he thinks about
taking the sweater off.

*Seven years from the day she
finishes her long dying, he visits
the zoo. Throngs of pregnant women,
families pushing children in strollers
watch a polar bear nurse a cub.
Her dreamy eyes as the cub sucks;
the soles of her splayed paws
like white socks stained with mud.*

In seven years each atom
shifts, each cell's replaced;
in seven years new teeth,
new feet, new friends.
Whole cities built, rebuilt
brick by brick, block by block.

*Sometimes, even many years
later, mending fences
others broke down.*

Everyone knows how grief
washes a man's face in the morning,
rocks him to sleep at night.
Yet nothing lasts, not even grief.

Not three weeks after I marry her widowed father, my new

—what? "stepdaughter"? "husband's daughter"?—jumps
from a plane in New Zealand without asking anyone's
permission though if she did it wouldn't be mine anyway,
making this rush of *–anger? compassion? envy?—*
for a twenty-year-old woman not technically my child
nothing I know what to do with but feel it, along with relief
that by the time the news reaches us in Chicago she's
safely back on the ground sending emails describing
how her neck felt as she fell, something between "flabby"
and "flattened"*—how could it be anger?—*and meanwhile
there's the irony of that postage stamp I chose for our
wedding invitations, a commemorative honoring Harriet
Quimby, first American female licensed pilot, back when
I thought of Harriet as representing us taking off
for unknown skies, well before we learned from an exhibit
at a Colorado regional airport how the real Harriet,
herself never married, fell from a plane and died, leaving
her parents heartbroken—*no, not quite envy, either*—though
in the first weeks of this, my second, marriage I'll have
moments believing that flight may be my best option, as
when that updraft of desire I feel for him the night after
I move my things into—*their? his?*—house, nothing gentle,
lifts me into air too thin to breathe and I flee down snowy
streets in my blue car singing *Goodbye yellow brick high
school, Goodbye ice cream shop,* not knowing exactly
where I will land, or when, or that, waking beside him
the next morning, I'll think to send her an only slightly
scolding postcard which won't reach her for weeks if ever
and we'll grope our way forward, somehow family now—

When We Were a Holy Family

Those were the happy times,
before little brother was born.
The three of us in the kitchen
at breakfast time, Father
reading yesterday's cricket scores,

Shiva stirring khichri,
asking nothing for herself,
not even a place to sit—and I,
Kartikya, gold-toothed, bright-
colored, born of the river Ganges,

seated in the high chair, not a spot
of saliva marking my bib, the one
with the choo-choo train motif…

Of course parents will want more,
of course conflict will ensue,
but why *Ganesha?* why the horrible
accident of *that one*'s babyhood,
centering all attention on *him*?

Why my relocation to the straight-
backed chair, *Ganesha* now elevated,
angelic tusks shining, astonishing trunk
curled around a sugar plum dessert?

Were we not still the same family,
Shiva, Parvathi, and me?
–No one has ever apologized for this.

Why We Rejected Our Stepmother

I

Because she gave us the wrong presents on the wrong holidays.
Because she sang "Happy Birthday" wrong.
Because sometimes she signed letters to us using the "L" word
and sometimes not.

Because she ate four of the cookies
our aunt mailed to us from North Carolina,
after Dad offered them to her.
Because she blamed her fart on Mom's dog, in Mom's kitchen,
where we had not offered her any of our guacamole anyway,

and sat in our places at the breakfast table
when we were home after summer camp
with only a few days to sit in them ourselves
before we went back to college.

Because she made Dad happy in ways we couldn't,
in ways even Mom couldn't any more,
and that made us sad.

II

To be honest there were things we liked about her,
though we disagreed about which ones and how much.

Like, that she didn't have a job, so she could help Dad
around the house, giving him more time to spend
with us. At first that seemed like a good thing,

even if she moved Mom's clothes and wigs and hats,
the baby clothes Mom had saved in the attic for our babies,
and every other thing we liked leaving in the places Mom left them.

III

There were many more things we disliked, though,
and we agreed on almost all of these.

Like, that she moved into our house and put her things
in the living room and the basement and Dad's bedroom,

that she slept with Dad in the bed Mom had slept in with Dad,
and sat on the couch with Dad in the room where Mom died,
and on the living room couch, in front of the fireplace,
where we wanted to be alone with Dad,

that she could see us on our video calls with Dad even
if we didn't look directly at her (which we didn't),

that she ate meat, behind our backs, with Dad,
and when we told Dad it was disgusting he told us for the first time
that Mom had once eaten veal,
which he obviously said just to protect her,

IV

that she did not adequately fear either Dad or us,

that after we finished college, Dad sold our house
to buy another one with her,
and since we didn't have our own rooms in Dad's new house,
we had to move some of our things into storage,

that her germs were not our germs, her viral load
not our viral load,
and even if she never touched us,
she touched Dad, which was bad enough,

that although she didn't look or smell or sound like Mom,
her being there made it hard for us to remember
how Mom looked and smelled and sounded,

that we wanted Mom back and even if that was impossible,
her being there made it more impossible.

Time Share at the Dells

Snowed in, roads iced over, we're stuck
one more night in an indoor waterpark,
bobbing inert in plastic inner tubes
until the buff lifeguard turns on the surf
throwing us headlong into tattooed dads,

tweens in polkadot bikinis. Back in
our unit, you switch on the flat-screen, cruise
for news, a weather break, but find only
reruns of "The Twilight Zone" on every
channel, back to back. We can't avoid

watching stars long since dead crash barriers
of space and time, science and fiction: Jack
Klugman racks up and breaks for Jonathan
Winters, in *an enchanted poolroom where
a middle-aged salesman has made a deal*

with Death. –I click the set off, and we walk
a maze of towel-strewn hallways for hot wings
and beers at the Thirsty Buffalo saloon,
then return to find the screen's turned itself on,
and a young Shatner's feigning thirst somewhere

in Utah. This time we aren't surprised
to hear Serling announce *his wrecked spaceship
never left Planet Earth*—only bug-eyed
from traveling to days of black and white,
when middle-aged was what we'd never be.

How I Save My Husband's Life

He's dead asleep at 4 AM the day
after my bunion surgery when I
climb out of bed to pee, rising too fast,
and pass out in the bathroom, landing slumped
against the tub, waking him with a cry,
and he too rises, runs to the doorway
and catches sight of me, kneels at my head
distraught, cradles me like a mortician

until I wake and shout at him to call
9-1-1 and he runs into the dark
kitchen to find the phone and, faint from shock,
trips over the rocker and falls, tearing
his rotator cuff so I have to call
my own damned ambulance—but it's all right,

sweetheart: as our team wails into ER
(your arm dangling, mine hooked up to saline),
it's not the EMT's firm biceps, lush
dark eyelashes, no, it's your pale grimace
that cheers me, it's your clammy hand I grip,
secure, knowing I'll have to stick around,
shouting orders and keeping you on task.

Psalm 2000

King David loiters outside Zion Gate
strumming a wooden harp, singing words
of ancient invention: *Hosanna, Hear
O Israel.* Tourists toss shekels at
his dirty feet. Behind the horsehair beard
he's hot, but a breeze sneaks up his skirt.

Last night he dozed off on his daughter's couch,
TV still blaring news. He can't stay long—
he'll find his own digs now Bathsheba's gone.
Tomorrow he'll try Acco: take the bus,
join other pilgrims looking for his truth.
In spotted daylight, by the ruined baths,
he'll sing doo-wop, guitar line bouncing off
blue-glazed tiles: *why do fools fall in love?*

After seeing our retirement advisor, I fall asleep

and dream we're Hobbits
dressed in the style of our immigrant ancestors.
Tomorrow you'll fly to New York to visit

the married daughter who won't speak to me
so we spend tonight balancing checkbooks,
subtracting credit card bills,

shocking ourselves with our extravagance. At this rate
there'll be nothing for the grandkids
but my ancient Seiko travel alarm

with its broken second hand, and that
only if I give up Starbucks
and you die at your desk.

I search my rag bundle for gold
as the Seiko chimes, reminding me I'm old.

To My Father, From a Stopped Ski Lift

Wherever you are now, it's not behind
that Ponderosa pine draped with purple
Mardi Gras beads and frozen lace brassieres,
not over that rise, not inside that puff
of morning fog. I'm not the type to hear
voices, feel presences in sudden chills,
though sometimes I dream of people I

don't recognize who might (might not) be you.
At this moment, dangling mid-air, I watch
one skier pick a cautious path cross-hill.
He's tall, as you were; stooped, ready
to fall. He even wears your frayed blue
ski jacket, red stocking cap. How can
I bear this silence, bear to reach the top

and head downhill without you? Yes, I know
I don't need you to rouse me in half-light,
lace my ski boots, rub my small fingers
between your big hands, to give me one
last lesson in ski math, how a ten-buck pass
divided by five runs makes two dollars
per run so we can't stop yet, not until

it's dark and I'm too tired to drink my hot
chocolate. Yet watching an old man ski
I long to catch him, take his arm, ask him
if he remembers that white-out in Zermatt,
the time you lost, then found me
waiting for you beside the little bridge,
the time we caught the last train back to town.

Halloween, San Francisco

Between the modern art museum and the Mexican-
Indonesian-Thai-Turkish-Vietnamese
luncheonette where for a second day I eat
greasy pork kabobs and bland

noodles, a man on the sidewalk slumps
over a cardboard sign that yesterday
read "Famished" and today says "Ravenous."
Moving closer I see he's not asleep

but reading *Us*, the topmost in a stack
behind his sign. It's tricky here, sorting
what's real from what isn't. Mickey walks by,
blood gushing from a head wound. A geisha

hangs off a cable car. Zombie brides play
speed chess on Market Street, ogled by stoned
gold prospectors, Vietnam vets with flags
duct-taped to stolen grocery carts. Today

the Pentagon put everyone on high alert,
not saying what that meant. Nervous
shop owners shut their metal gates early.
A man wrapped in a tattered blanket stops

sorting through garbage cans to flutter it
at a pair of chattering teens, shouts "Boo!"
then returns to humming "Born to be Wild."
Real, not real? No matter. It's how he feels.

Tight Wire

Something's bugging him. Could it be me,
straining to keep my voice level and warm
as I guard the food pantry swap table?
"Wait til you get your bag, then anything
you don't want, you'll swap. Up to two items,"
I warn. His eyes flash fire. Is it PTSD,

raging delusion, non-prescription drugs?
He wanders back and forth, watching. "Did you
see that?" he says. "That person there traded
four cans of corn." When his bag comes, he takes
a full half hour to pack his food into
his camo backpack. He takes out a box

of macaroni, sets it down, swaps it
for canned peas. Puts them in, takes them out,
trades a loaf of bread. I'm trying not to count,
even let on I'm watching though maybe

that's what he wants—to be counted, noticed.
Now everything's out, spread across three chairs
and a table: bread, fresh carrots, two cans
of chicken stew. "Is there a problem?" I'm

smiling, trying hard not to condescend.
"How about some fresh raspberries?" I hold
them out to him as he dives for the door,
eyes panicky: "I got a train to catch."

I figure that's the last I'll see of him
but then he's back, defiant, summoning
all his will to pack his food in a box,
all his courage to carry it away.

October

This round month,
month of empty mouths
and still no snow:

in the plucked garden
a rabbit wanders in circles,
looks for the dog
who lived here once.

A month to try on old clothes
before settling for basic
black and white. On the parkway
maples in red stocking caps;

gaunt elms, naked but for
moth-chewed argyle socks;
oaks in ragged brown
overcoats, and gingkoes

shaking off yellow sweaters,
covering lawns in the dog-eared
lost poems of trees.

The Gods Create Heavy Weather

God said "From this one tree you may not eat,"
then hitched His horse up for a buggy ride.
It was unseemly warm for March, the heat
had burst the blooms of Heaven's magnolias wide,
fried Mrs. G's jonquils, while down below,
Earth's baseball teams sweated through training camp.
And Lo, there came a hole in the ozone,
God's carriage wheel dipped and bent, His cell phone

flew from His hand, and Mrs. G knew Eve
(couldn't be Adam), oh yes, Eve had done
something extra naughty this time, like ship
her toxic e-waste offshore to be stripped
of rare earth metals by bare-naked kids.
So God said "Let there be messy weather,"
and Mrs. God said "Call it 'climate change.'"
And so it was. And there came hail, and rain,

and angry birds, and earthquakes, fire and frost,
and on Opening Day, such ice and storms
Earth's catchers could not see their mitts before
their masks. And every tender white and pink
blossom of all Earth's fruiting trees turned black,
frost killed the fragrant heralds of Her pears
and apples, plums and apricots, Her Old
King Davids and Her Maiden Blush,
Her Pippins. Her old trees withered and died,
and everywhere on Earth the farmers cried.

Mayday

All of a sudden it's hail like baby
        teeth dropping out of the blue
                sky, then bigger, like elderly gents', at last

like horses' molars clattering
        clop clop clop on the scaffolding clamped
                like orthodontia over the doorway of the American

Dental Association. Maxillofacial surgeons in sleeveless
        floral-print dresses and high heels clutch
                useless umbrellas, clump

like wilted coleus under the portico while tie-dyed
        periodontists leap the curb,
                smash ice-balls on marble.

Tulips planted yesterday in sidewalk sarcophagi
        shed petals, become soldierly rows
                of naked stems. A disoriented

taxi driver backs past us, hazards flashing, as a robin
        flies low, grazes the doorman's lush hair.
                It's what we Chicago dentists call "spring."

The Rain Woman

—after Wallace Stevens "The Snow Man"

She must have a body of city
to dig Motown and the moan
of Firestones painted with mud;

and have been homeless for centuries
to feel the Lincolns whining for oil,
the semis loud in the near muffle

of the West Side; and not to glean
any comfort from the heat of the sun,
from the heat of a trash fire,

which is the heat of engines
full of the same sun
that is shining on the same hard face

of the panhandler, who panhandles on the off ramp,
and, woman herself, feels
woman who is not there and the woman who is.

Morning on Mars

Here on Mars there's nothing much to do
but wander from one yellow rock to another,
from one bottomless ravine to another,

always looking down. I'm
constantly surprised by sunrise,
by the return of loneliness I never felt

receding. Every morning starts
with whistling silence, enough
to freeze one to death if one were not

already deathly cold. Ah! for the smell
of a horse, for a clean pair
of flannel pajamas!

Yang

There's nothing womanish about me. When I'm
a man, I walk right in, no "Knock-knock," no
"Yoo-hoo, anybody home?" I step right up, slap
my two bucks on the counter, grab all three
baseballs in one hand, I wind up and let fly.
When I'm a man, I hoist myself into the chair,
smack bootheel to wrought iron, say "The usual,
Tony." I cross LaSalle Street, halting traffic
with an outstretched hand, and all the buildings—
Monadnock, Sears Tower, John Hancock—look just
like me. When I get where I'm going, a receptionist
with red fingernails will ask me twice whether
it's Stephen with a "ph" or a "v." It's like
she's from another species—a mynah bird, say,
or some kind of endangered big cat. When I'm a man,
I make war, not love. There's always someone waiting
to hear from me, never time to call. It's a shave,
a shower, and I'm back at the wheel, on the air,
behind the lawn mower. Dogs scatter when I'm a man.
It's a day's work just carrying my shoulders around.

Seven Ways of Listening to a Crow

1. Outside the post office
      the sound of a crow
            hopping on one leg.

2. If a crow caws in the forest
      and no one hears it
            could it have been a blackbird?

3. Crows gather, flapping
      over the children's
            hospital.

4. The rattle of dice
      in a wood cup
            ends the crow's call.

5. The primacy of sight
      is nothing to a blind
            crow.

6. A city is too loud
      for blackbirds, not loud enough
            for crows.

7. Clouseau with a shotgun
      game warden looks suspicious
            fallen from fir tree, crow says nothing.

Mrs. Buddha Calls on Mrs. God

"Tea or coffee?" asks Mrs. God, hopeful
for an excuse to fire up her brand new
espresso machine, a gift from Mr. God
last Christmas—he said it was from Santa,
their little joke. Mrs. Buddha can't
decide. "So many ways to burn water!"
she marvels, wondering if it's polite
to marvel here in Heaven. Certainly
it would be bad form back in Nirvana

but everything's so different here—why,
outside the front gate, didn't she just see
a billboard instructing her to Choose Life?
("What's that about?" she wondered.) Still,
no question it gets boring back home: each day
the same, no rebirths, no red eggs and ginger,
no—*you* know—fireworks. Sometimes
she finds herself dreaming of one more turn

dressed in the clothes of skin and bone,
imagining the new unmet desires, diseases,
deaths a destiny as Dragon or Dog
might bring. She'd miss her Mr. B, but he'd
be fine. She'd leave him plenty of tea-cakes
to renounce—pumpkin spice, zucchini,
imported Madagascar vanilla—like those her new
friend proffers now, with a cool glass of cider,
fresh-pressed from fruit right off the tree.

Square One

Let's say I'm a cardboard box with great legs.
I'm twenty-eight, life's hollow, and the tick-
tock of my baby clock has me on edge.
Where do I go to find my parallel, my nick,

my Mr. Right—at least Mr. Right Angle—that cool zir-
conium-in-the-rough who will assuage
my A-times-B-times-C-sized emptiness? Forget last year.
That travel agent sent me far astray

to visit the Pyramids. (What was she thinking?) I
fell from the felluca, got hammered at the Hilton bar, and not
one blockhead's sidewise glance, even in my
peek-a-boo yashmak. This summer I'll be hot

in Mesa. I'll show off my gams, outline my lips.
I'll know him by his Prairie style shoulders, bungalow hips.

Sunrise at the Busy Bee Cafe

Since four o'clock, in their hive thrumming
with fluorescent lamps, women have worked,
twined braids pinned up like crowns, pale
strong hands rolling paler dough
for *pierogi*, pressing water glasses

to cut perfect disks, dabbing dots of mashed
potato, mushroom paste, plum jam. Fragrance
of allspice, prune and vinegar as *czarnina*
simmers on a steady flame. From a radio,
turned down, a man's voice reads Polish news.

Overhead, a Blue Line train growls northwest
to southeast into the Loop. Now the sun
marks the horizon with a narrow line,
pushes dark sky away from darker lake
until there's light—barely enough—to guide

men across Milwaukee Avenue, each one
carrying an empty thermos. They mass
along the plate glass with a murmur of
dzien dobry, good morning, for one another
and for the grill cook who unlocks the door,

lets them in. Backlit, they flow across linoleum,
take places at the counter where fried eggs
appear, then coffee, slices of white bread
coated with butter, sprinkling of salt. Under
the color portrait of John Paul, they chew

and idly watch through an open doorway
as the high school girl sets a white doily down
on each small table in the dining room.
One man thinks of—what was her name?
So long ago, a continent away, he's forgotten

much. By the time he'll stub out
his cigarette, light fills the sky, and soon
it's blinding. Nothing to do for now
but close his eyes, inhale, and think of—
nowhere. Of wild green ducks, flying home.

Jesus Heads Home

> *"Then the page someone folded to mark her page.*
> *Then the page on which nothing happens.*
> *The page after this page. ..."*
> —Srikanth Reddy, "Burial Practice," in *Facts for Visitors*

On the evening train, holding an open book
she watches as a man two rows ahead

eats barbecue, licks his fingers, wipes them
with a brown napkin, wipes the same damp scrap
across his mouth. The West Side rattles past.

Economy of spit, of brown paper:
not everything sells in an options pit.

Blue skies with wisps of maize, wisps of red smoke
rising from factories to the southwest
don't trade on three-month contracts. Nor
does death. Closing her eyes, she tries to imagine

her last moment, then the moment after that
moment: the page after this page, the world
continuing, the oak growing another ring.

She lets go of light, taste, touch, tries to release
kinesthesia but finds herself still
captive, still praying: *not now, not here; not*
this light, not this air; not this dark platform

over this city street. Wait, she prays, *wait*
until the man's walked past, trailing his greasy napkin,
his sweet smell of ironed pants, grilled meat.

Short Cut

    —in memoriam Dean Young (1955-2022)

"Begin by taking the road marked
        NO THROUGH TRAFFIC,"

says the golden-haired boy,
        bucket of deck stain in one hand,
                dripping paintbrush in the other.

"Though more hilly, it is
        the quickest way to get from here to there,

especially if you don't have a car.
        Walk past the signs that say

PRIVATE,
        KEEP OUT,
                NO TRESPASSING,

the one that says
        FLYING TRAPEZE LESSONS THIS WAY
                              —didn't you say

you're in a hurry? Keep walking.
        You'll come to a sign with a bent black arrow
                slashed by a thinner line, meaning 'no left turn.'

Turn left. Here—put these stale
        bread crusts in your pockets. You may

need them. Ignore the barking dog, the sign that says
        ROAD ENDING.

Crawl under the pig-iron gate—this
        is when not having a car comes in handy.

Continue downhill—you're almost there now.
        Across the slippery rocks, keep your shoes on,
                and keep walking. Keep walking. Keep walking."

Dark Night

O sharp-edged poem, square-headed,
unrepentant: in giving birth to you
I sustain further damage.

In bearing you, awkward, malformed
lines, my unhappy womb
stretches into ever more grotesque

shapes, the edges of my mouth
rip and bleed.
You emerge at the wrong time

and place: back seat of a taxicab,
deserted cornfield in the dead
of winter. Uncalled, uncalled-for

child disowned by your father,
you leave me bloody,
cracked and resewn. Yet you

are all the child I'll ever have;
grateful, I press your hard mouth
to my breast.

Notes

"Bazooka Joe Fantasies" is based on the Bazooka™ brand bubble gum comic, "Bazooka Joe Fantasies Comic #34 of 50" (artist unknown)

"Square One" refers to a black and white photograph from the joint studio of Barb Ciurej and Lindsay Lochman (Milwaukee, 1983).

"To My Period" is an homage to Kenneth Koch's *New Addresses* (Knopf, 2001), a collection of apostrophes, and particularly to his "To My Twenties."

Acknowledgments

Grateful acknowledgement is made to the following publications where versions of some of the poems in this book were first published:

After Bei Dao, The Evil Eye, Forgiveness, and Gristle in *Rhino*

American Air, Halloween, San Francisco, Hooked (as "Hookup") and Outside the AIDS Ward in *Sanskrit*

Apples to Apples, Bazooka Joe Fantasies, Fill-'er-Up, How Not to Drown, Jesus Heads Home, Mayday, Morning on Mars, October, On El Greco's "Assumption of the Virgin" (1627), Square One, Sunrise at the Busy Bee Café, and Survivor in *After Hours*

At the Front in HerMark, WomanMade Gallery (Chicago) 2001 calendar

Barbershop, Boy Crazy, Grad School/Iraq (as "Junior Year"), Love and War, Not three weeks after I marry her widowed father, my new, To My Father, From a Stopped Ski Lift, and Wedding in *Willow Review*

Baseline Scan (as "Michigan Ave 2003") in *Spoon River Poetry Review*

Constant Comment in *I Will Bear This Scar: Poems of Childless Women* (iUniverse, 2005)

Dark Night in *Folio*

How I Save My Husband's Life, Like Botox for the Brain and Mrs. Buddha Calls on Mrs. God in */nor*

Illinois in *Where We Live: Illinois Poets* (BookSurge Publishing, 2003)

Listening to OCD, Midwinter Holiday, New Snow and That Lonesome Hallway in *Buckle&*

My Older Sister Teaches Me to Read in *Cimarron*

Running Wild and Who Needs a Heart (as "Days of 1985") in *Poetry East*

Seven Ways of Listening to a Crow and What We Stand For in *Evening Street Review*

The Gods Create Heavy Weather in *Escape Into Life*

The Truth About Jesus and Windowshopping at the Pink Elephant in *River Oak Review*

Time Share at the Dells, as Honorable Mention in *Naugatuck River Review* Narrative Poetry Contest

To My Period in *Body: landscape/mindscape, a collaborative experiment of the arts* (The Fuzion Project, Chicago, 2003)

Yang in *Third Coast*

Patricia McMillen is a retired lawyer, folk musician and clown-in-becoming. When she started writing poetry as an adult, her teacher Maureen Seaton encouraged the class to write about their obsessions, so it is relevant to note that her current obsessions include time and light. Prior to completing the manuscript of this, her first full-length poetry collection, her proudest accomplishments in life were negotiating the 2005 sale of 1000 acres of family-owned Illinois farmland to The Nature Conservancy, doubling the size of TNC's Nachusa Grasslands and permitting it to become the present home of Illinois' first bison herd; joining the movement that successfully advocated for Illinois' abolition of capital punishment in 2011, including dedicating a poetry chapbook, *Knife Lake Anthology* (Columbus, OH: Pudding House Publications 2006) to the effects of state-sanctioned murder on a small semi-fictional community; and becoming an adult Bat Mitzvah (Daughter of the Law) in 2015, at Oak Park (Illinois)' Reform Jewish synagogue, Oak Park Temple.

www.ingramcontent.com/pod-product-compliance
Lightning Source LLC
Chambersburg PA
CBHW020338170426
43200CB00006B/425